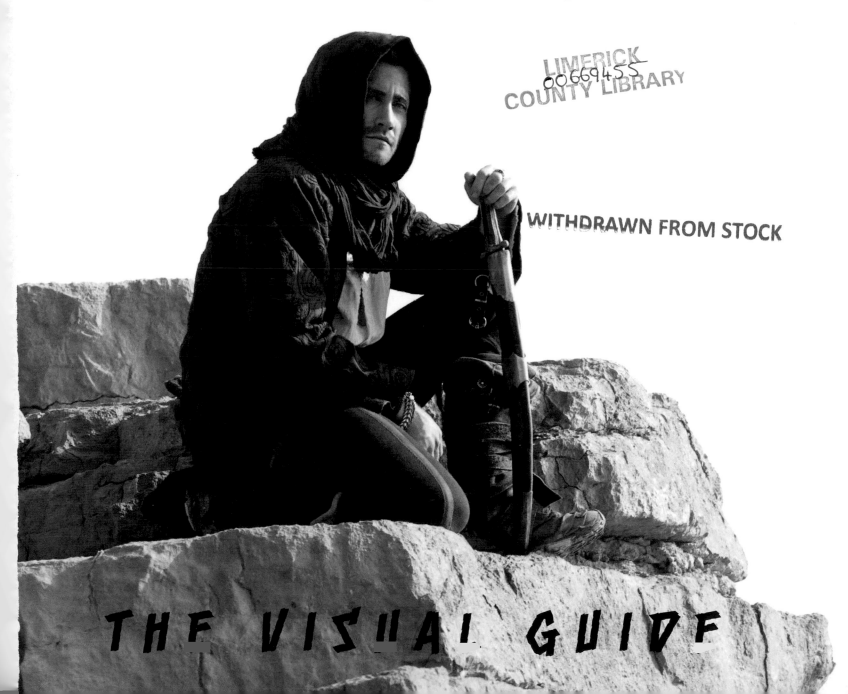

PRINCE OF PERSIA
THE SANDS OF TIME

THE VISUAL GUIDE

FOREWORD

A great deal of sand has passed through the hourglass since a film has been made using the wonderfully magical and colourful world of the ancient 'Near East' as a backdrop. Previous generations grew up watching film versions of spectacular fantasy adventures like *The Thief of Bagdad*, *Ali Baba and the Forty Thieves* and Ray Harryhausen's marvellous series that began with *The 7th Voyage of Sinbad*, not to mention the more realistic drama of David Lean's classic *Lawrence of Arabia*, but these wondrous and exotic tales of adventure have virtually vanished from the screen.

But in 1989, a brilliant young man named Jordan Mechner drew on the beauty and mythology of ancient Persia in the creation of a completely new kind of video game, which he titled 'Prince of Persia.' The original game is now a classic of the gamer world, and seemed to us an exciting foundation for a new feature fantasy adventure in which we could revive an entire genre, just as we did with the *Pirates of the Caribbean* films. In *Prince of Persia: The Sands of Time*, we've tried to raise the special world that Jordan conjured up in his games to a cinematic level with Mike Newell at the helm as director; Jake Gyllenhaal, Gemma Arterton, Ben Kingsley and Alfred Molina at the head of a marvellous cast in front of the camera; and thousands of other cast and crew members lending their heroic support throughout an incredibly arduous shoot in Morocco and London.

This new DK book gives you an all-access pass to the wonderful world of *Prince of Persia: The Sands of Time*, not only the story of the movie but also the amazing locations, characters, weapons and combat style. Hopefully you'll get a sense of the mind-boggling amount of work that went into the making of the film, even if you're not able to feel the 115 degree Fahrenheit temperatures that assailed us in Morocco, or swallow the grit that the fierce desert winds blew into our faces during occasional sandstorms.

Then again, we actually lived the adventure, and by turning the page, so will you!

Jerry Bruckheimer

CONTENTS

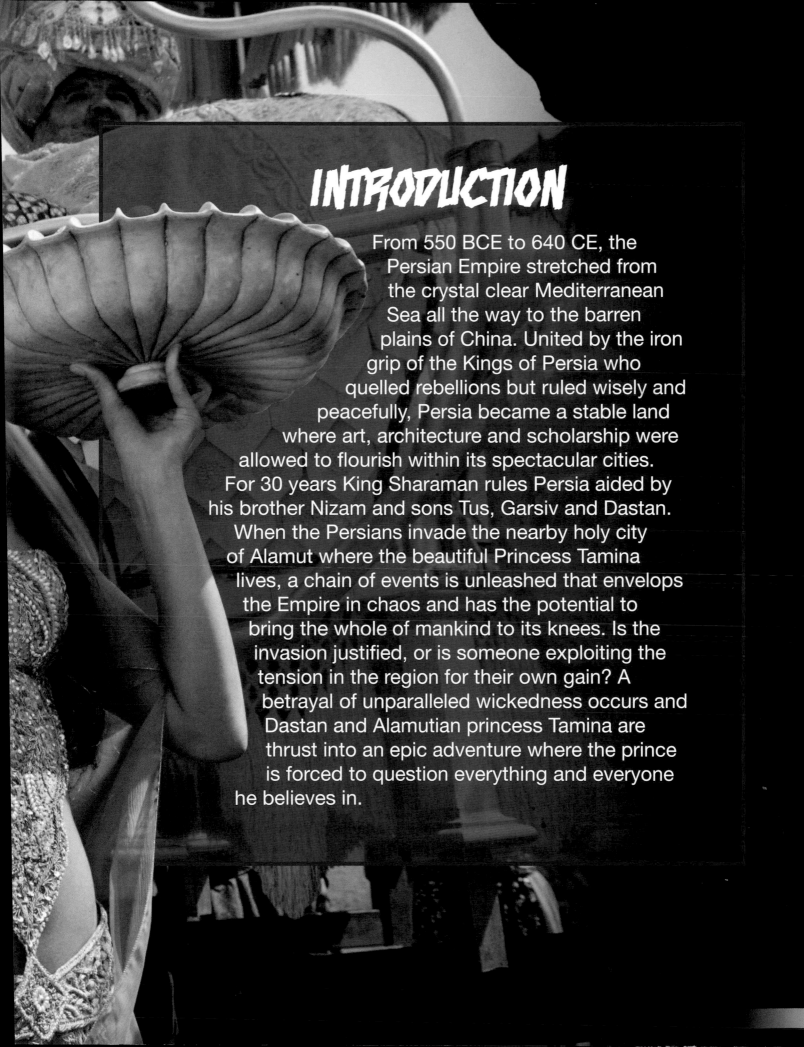

INTRODUCTION

From 550 BCE to 640 CE, the
Persian Empire stretched from
the crystal clear Mediterranean
Sea all the way to the barren
plains of China. United by the iron
grip of the Kings of Persia who
quelled rebellions but ruled wisely and
peacefully, Persia became a stable land
where art, architecture and scholarship were
allowed to flourish within its spectacular cities.
For 30 years King Sharaman rules Persia aided by
his brother Nizam and sons Tus, Garsiv and Dastan.
When the Persians invade the nearby holy city
of Alamut where the beautiful Princess Tamina
lives, a chain of events is unleashed that envelops
the Empire in chaos and has the potential to
bring the whole of mankind to its knees. Is the
invasion justified, or is someone exploiting the
tension in the region for their own gain? A
betrayal of unparalleled wickedness occurs and
Dastan and Alamutian princess Tamina are
thrust into an epic adventure where the prince
is forced to question everything and everyone
he believes in.

THE PERSIAN EMPIRE

ALTHOUGH DASTAN AND TAMINA GO ON AN EPIC journey through the desert from Alamut to Avrat, in fact the cities are close together. They are positioned near the Silk Road, marked on this map by a red line. This trade route, which connected China to the Mediterranean, was the artery for the region. It not only brought a flow of wealth to the area but also culture and knowledge. It helped the Persian Empire to be at the centre of the world between East and West, spreading its influences way beyond the edges of this map.

BLACK SEA

Antioch

THE SILK ROAD

SYRIA

MEDITERRANEAN SEA

ARABIA

Persia's territory includes barren deserts and rocky wastelands that make it hard to travel long distances. The difficult terrain also reflects the tensions in the region, as Persia has been engaged in a war with the province of Koshkahn for many years.

RED SEA

CASPIAN SEA

Merv

Hecatompylos

AVRAT

NASAF

Hamadan

PERSIA

ALAMUT

The Alamutians are based in the sacred city of Alamut and the Persians are located in the capital of Persia, Nasaf.

Basra

PERSIAN GULF

Siraf

TWO KINGDOMS

THERE HAS ALWAYS BEEN PEACE BETWEEN THE PERSIAN Empire and the sacred city of Alamut, which is located on the farthest edge of the region. However, relations have now been threatened since rumours began circulating that the kingdom of Alamut is conspiring against the Persians and harbouring weapons for the Koshkahn with whom Persia is at war. The Persians have responded to the rumours by sending armies to camp outside Alamut. The forces are led by Prince Tus and accompanied by Sharaman's brother Nizam, Prince Garsiv and Prince Dastan. The King has ordered that they must never invade the city.

RUMOURS AND LIES

The rumours of Alamut's moves against Persia are entirely false. They have been spread by Nizam. With the Persian forces poised on the edge of the city, the final stage of Nizam's plot falls into place. He plants evidence that Alamut is secretly producing and sending weapons to arm the Kosh warlords fighting Persia. Soon one of his spies conveniently 'discovers' the evidence. What Nizam really wants is to sieze the magical Dagger of Time, kept in Alamut, to allow him ultimate control.

THE BATTLE OF ALAMUT

Presented with Nizam's new evidence and urged on by his uncle, Tus gives the order to attack against his father's wishes. Eager to impress, Dastan and a small band of men scale one of the city walls and against orders manage to open the Eastern Gate to let the Persian forces in. Taking the Alamutian forces by surprise, the battle is bloody and brutally efficient. The Persians quickly enter the city and a new era begins.

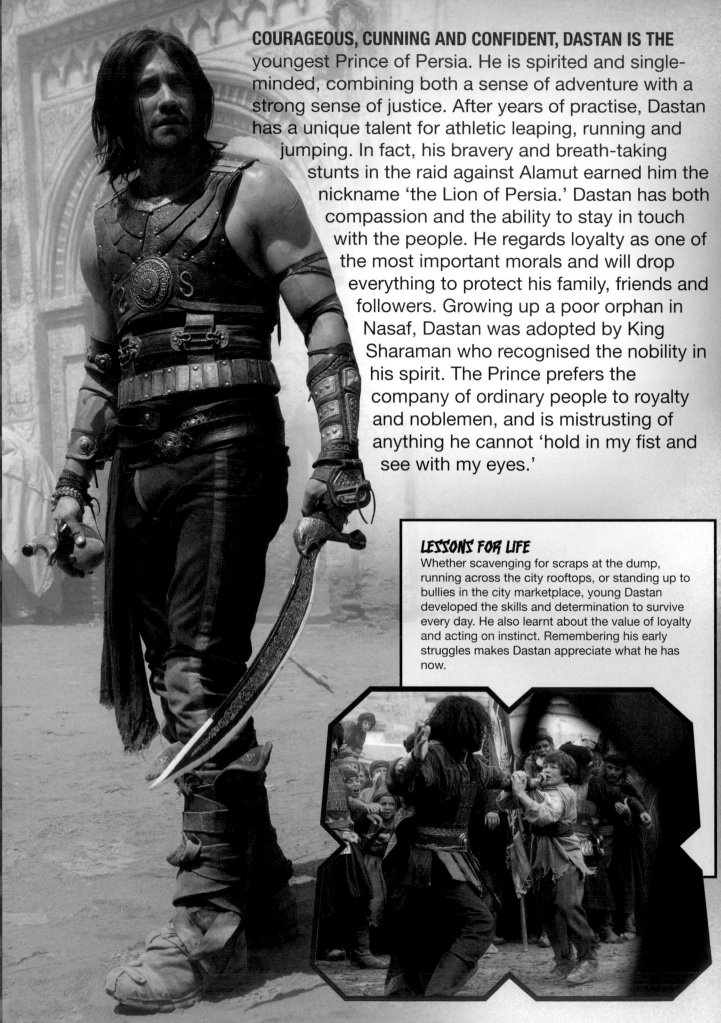

COURAGEOUS, CUNNING AND CONFIDENT, DASTAN IS THE youngest Prince of Persia. He is spirited and single-minded, combining both a sense of adventure with a strong sense of justice. After years of practise, Dastan has a unique talent for athletic leaping, running and jumping. In fact, his bravery and breath-taking stunts in the raid against Alamut earned him the nickname 'the Lion of Persia.' Dastan has both compassion and the ability to stay in touch with the people. He regards loyalty as one of the most important morals and will drop everything to protect his family, friends and followers. Growing up a poor orphan in Nasaf, Dastan was adopted by King Sharaman who recognised the nobility in his spirit. The Prince prefers the company of ordinary people to royalty and noblemen, and is mistrusting of anything he cannot 'hold in my fist and see with my eyes.'

LESSONS FOR LIFE

Whether scavenging for scraps at the dump, running across the city rooftops, or standing up to bullies in the city marketplace, young Dastan developed the skills and determination to survive every day. He also learnt about the value of loyalty and acting on instinct. Remembering his early struggles makes Dastan appreciate what he has now.

FATHER AND SON

When Dastan was adopted by Sharaman, he went straight from life on the streets to the lavish luxuries of the royal palace. Taking this giant leap in his stride, Dastan has developed a powerful bond with the King as strong as any father and son. Dastan is always eager to earn his father's respect, although Sharaman believes his youngest son still has some growing up to do.

PRINCE MEETS PRINCESS

When Prince Dastan meets Princess Tamina he is amazed to meet a woman who is more than a match for him. Although they start off as foes and she thinks he has the manners of a camel, their feisty and sometimes fiery relationship suggests there is some chemistry!

DUAL PERSONALITY

Whether using a weapon, or fighting hand to hand, Dastan's lightning reactions and fighting instinct means he can outfox almost anyone in one-on-one combat. Dastan is a brave warrior who can anticipate his opponent's every move. He loves to be tested, whether it is by defeating his enemies or by sparring with his own men for fun!

DASTAN AND THE DAGGER

When Dastan finds the mysterious Dagger of Time, he realises it has incredible powers. The find is a catalyst not just for the catastrophic events and incredible adventures that happen around Alamut but also his own personal journey to discover just who he is and what he is to become.

THE APPLE INCIDENT

IT IS AMAZING HOW ONE INCIDENT CAN CHANGE THE COURSE OF history. When King Sharaman happens to witness ten-year-old Dastan's selfless act of bravery, it transforms Dastan's life. Finding out that Dastan is an orphan, Sharaman chooses to adopt him as the third Prince of Persia. Some might call it a coincidence, whilst others might argue its part of Dastan's destiny. One thing is for sure, the events that take place on that day in Nasaf's marketplace have profound consequences for Dastan and for Persia.

For the young Dastan, the dusty rooftops of Nasaf are like an enormous obstacle course. Knowing the contours and corner of every building, he runs and leaps from roof to roof, delivering messages and parcels as he speeds through the city.

DELIVERING THE GOODS
The bustling marketplace square in Nasaf is famous throughout the Kingdom. With traders travelling along the Silk Road, it is always packed with people. When young Dastan delivers a parcel there, he decides to enjoy the fruits of his labour by spending his money on a rare treat – a juicy apple from one of the market stores.

Dastan is incensed when he sees his friend Yusef being struck by an army captain. He feels compelled to act and do something to help immediately!

GOOD SHOT!
When Dastan yells at the captain to stop and throws his apple at him, an amused and astonished crowd gathers to watch a young boy stand up to an army officer. Tripping the captain up, Dastan is able to rescue Yusef and escape into the rooftops. However, a roof gutter collapses and Dastan falls, finding a livid captain intent on cutting his hand off with his sword!

A HELPING HAND

Just as Dastan is about to be punished, King Sharaman appears. The whole marketplace bows their heads in deference. Only Dastan stands and stares the King in the face. Having witnessed the entire incident, Sharaman is deeply affected by the way Dastan stood up for what he thought was right.

A KING IN SPIRIT

Many years later Sharaman declares 'I saw a boy whose blood wasn't noble, but whose character was. A king in spirit!' In the market, Sharaman had seen a glimpse of the greatness that Dastan was capable of and convinced himself that he should take this orphan in from the streets to be the third Prince of Persia.

KING SHARAMAN

RULING OVER PERSIA FOR MORE THAN FORTY years, Sharaman is *Shah-ah-Shah*, the King of Kings. He is a true statesman who recognises the responsibilities of a ruler, and commands great respect from those close to him. Using a combination of wise government and ruthless force against dissenters, he has been able to maintain peace within Persia's fragile borders. However, now an older man, the King's priorities have changed and he is anxious to pave the way for a smooth succession for his sons. Sharaman has exceptionally high standards for them and he knows Tus and Garsiv are not yet ready for their royal roles and still have a lot to learn.

THE LION AND THE LIES

As a young boy, Sharaman's brother, Nizam, saved his life by killing a lioness when they were out hunting together. The incident has shaped Sharaman ever since and he has always trusted his younger brother and valued his judgement. Sharaman also strongly values brave deeds that display selfless loyalty rather than declarations and words.

TWO PRINCES

The arrival of Sharaman's first born son Tus, was greeted by celebrations throughout Nasaf and the entire Kingdom. As the cheers of the nobles in the great hall rang out, Sharaman felt elated the first time he held his son. The baby boy made him very proud and happy, and he was delighted that he now had an heir.

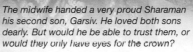

A KING AND A COMMANDER

As a young king, Sharaman was a brilliant military tactician, winning battles and invading territories. He expanded Persia's borders and also established peace. But forty years of rule have left him war-weary, and he now prefers prayer to the battlefield. Sharaman is absolutely furious when his sons attack Alamut against his wishes.

The midwife handed a very proud Sharaman his second son, Garsiv. He loved both sons dearly. But would he be able to trust them, or would they only have eyes for the crown?

THIRD TIME LUCKY

Sharaman never felt his family was quite complete and wanted a third son and heir. By adopting Dastan, he found a boy who embodied many of the qualities of loyalty and trust that he admired. Not only had he already witnessed Dastan's greatness, but with no ties of blood his new son would not covet the throne.

THE END OF THE REIGN

At a banquet in Alamut, the king is murdered and the whole Kingdom is thrust into mourning. It is not only his close family that are grief-stricken; thousands of people line the streets at his funeral in the city of Avrat. Their emotional outpourings and anger will last for a long time, but there is also the question of how to fill the enormous void left by Sharaman's death.

BETRAYAL

AFTER THE PERSIAN ARMY HAVE ENTERED Alamut, King Sharaman arrives unexpectedly from Nasaf furious that Tus has ordered the occupation against his express wishes. He has no idea that his journey will end in an act of such appalling treachery and disloyalty that it will not only tear the heart out of his family, but threaten the very foundations of the Kingdom. And for Dastan, the terrible events turn everything he has experienced on their head.

KIND WORDS
Although King Sharaman vents his anger at Tus, his dark mood is short-lived. Nizam organises a grand banquet in his brother's honour to be hold in the royal Palace at Alamut which helps to cool his anger. At the banquet, the King has fond words for Dastan, emphasising the great qualities that he has always seen in him.

THE BANQUET
With their goblets overflowing with wine, the assembled guests cheer emphatically as the Princes follow the Persian tradition of presenting a gift to their father. Whilst Tus is away trying to uncover Alamut's rumoured weapon forges, Garsiv presents the King with the booty and the severed heads of ten Koshkahn lords on behalf of both of them.

SHARAMAN'S ASSASSINATION

When Dastan presents the Regent of Alamut's prayer robe as a gift to Sharaman, the King immediately puts it on, but finds himself writhing in agonising pain! The robe has been poisoned, burning through to the skin of the wearer! As Sharaman's life comes to a rapid and untimely end, Dastan cradles his father's head in despair, whilst Garsiv accuses Dastan of murder. While Nizam plays the brother-in-mourning to perfection, he adds fuel to the fire by trying to persuade Tus and Garsiv to kill Dastan rather than seeking a trial.

ON THE RUN

With Dastan now effectively a fugitive, he is forced to flee. When Tamina realises that Dastan has the Dagger of Time she knows that she must stick with him, in the hope of recovering the weapon later. Because his brother first gave him the Regent's robe, Dastan believes Tus is the real murderer and has framed him. Dastan travels to Avrat to try to clear his name and to let his uncle know about Tus's guilt. It's not until he meets with Nizam that he realises he may be mistaken about the murderer's identity.

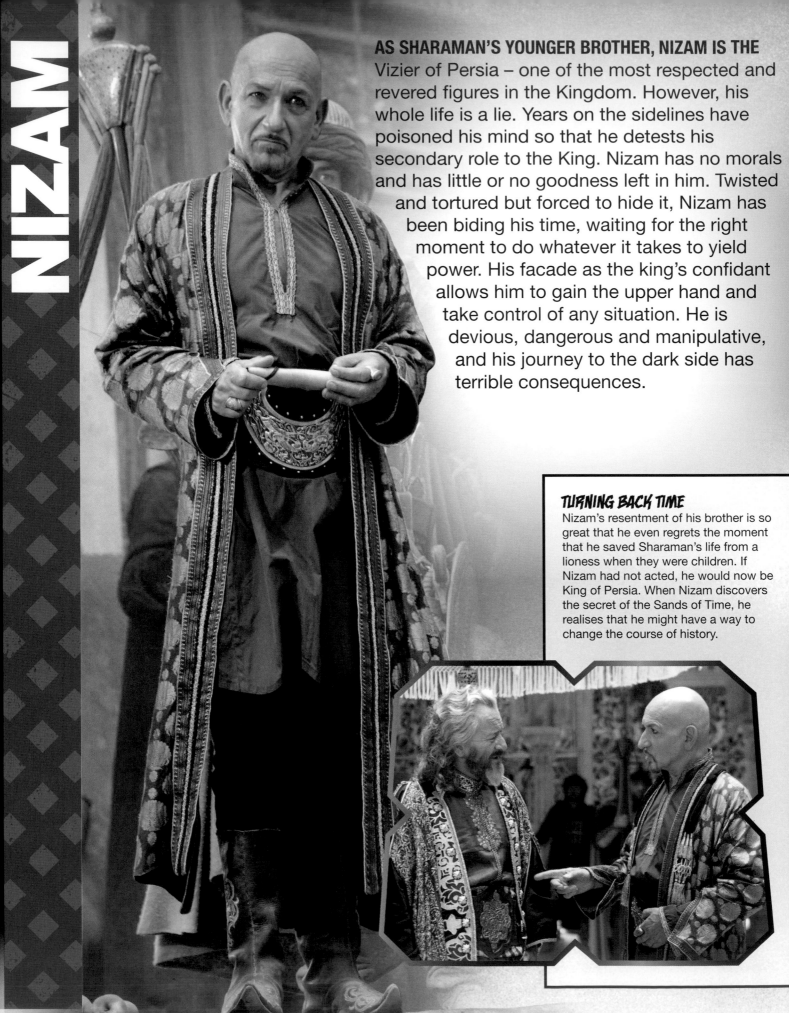

NIZAM

AS SHARAMAN'S YOUNGER BROTHER, NIZAM IS THE Vizier of Persia – one of the most respected and revered figures in the Kingdom. However, his whole life is a lie. Years on the sidelines have poisoned his mind so that he detests his secondary role to the King. Nizam has no morals and has little or no goodness left in him. Twisted and tortured but forced to hide it, Nizam has been biding his time, waiting for the right moment to do whatever it takes to yield power. His facade as the king's confidant allows him to gain the upper hand and take control of any situation. He is devious, dangerous and manipulative, and his journey to the dark side has terrible consequences.

TURNING BACK TIME
Nizam's resentment of his brother is so great that he even regrets the moment that he saved Sharaman's life from a lioness when they were children. If Nizam had not acted, he would now be King of Persia. When Nizam discovers the secret of the Sands of Time, he realises that he might have a way to change the course of history.

UNPLEASANT UNCLE

Dastan has always admired Nizam and regards him as a role model. Even after he has been framed for Sharaman's murder, Dastan looks to his uncle as the one person he can truly trust. For Nizam, Dastan is just a distraction. Once Nizam's treachery has been uncovered, the evil Vizier has no hesitation in encouraging Tus and Garsiv to get rid of Dastan.

THE VILE VIZIER

When Nizam attends his brother's funeral in the city of Avrat, the loathsome liar shows just how low he can go. Showing no remorse whatsoever, he draws on his impressive acting abilities. He pretends to be in deep mourning in front of thousands of people, leading Sharaman's coffin in the funeral procession and taking part in the ceremony.

HEAD OF THE HASSANSINS

The Hassansins are Nizam's hidden army of henchmen. These sadistic shadowy characters carry out all of Nizam's dirty work. Not only are the Hassansins responsible for his evil operations, they are also the source of his secret knowledge of the Sands of Time.

AS A CHILD, DASTAN GREW UP RUNNING FREE across and over the rooftops of Nasaf. After years of practise, he continues to use the same special skills in adulthood – leaping, jumping, running, falling, flipping, climbing, swinging, tumbling and landing – usually with pin-point accuracy and gravity-defying results! Depending on your point of view, Dastan is either fearless or foolish. His spectacular acrobatics and commando-style combat at breakneck speed are daring and deadly dangerous, but they can reap incredible results such as helping the fall of Alamut. Whatever happens, don't try this at home!

HEAD OVER HEELS

Some of Dastan's most impressive moves involve back flips, somersaults or dramatic falls that leave him upside-down. However, there is one thing that eludes Dastan – and it is driving him up the wall! As a child he was only ever able to do two steps in trying a vertical wall run, and as an adult he *still* can't seem to do that third step of the move.

LEAPS AND BOUNDS

It takes more than just physical prowess and skill to do all the amazing moves and manoeuvres that Dastan carries out. You also need incredible confidence in your abilities, intuition, discipline, a free-spirit and the odd bit of luck. Luckily, Dastan has these qualities in abundance and is the kind of guy who always seems to land on his feet!

DASTAN'S SPECIAL SKILLS

SPEED IS THE ESSENCE
Keeping up speed is vital to maintain momentum when jumping. Dastan has always been quick. As a child he was the fastest messenger in Nasaf.

ON THE REBOUND
Dastan's moves are always unpredictable. Leaping at a closed door then rebounding off not only fools a soldier at Avrat but also gives Dastan the extra power to knock him out.

ONWARDS AND UPWARDS
Dastan has always been deft at scrambling up the sheerest of walls, but scaling the perimeter of Alamut is a real challenge – especially when you're being fired at with arrows!

THINKING ON YOUR FEET
Take one vat of oil, a flaming torch, and a chain hoist and soon Dastan creates a wall of fire to repel the Alamutian forces, who he then avoids by swinging on the chain!

ROUND AND ROUND
Anything is a potential prop to help Dastan propel himself. At Avrat, he even uses the spike on top of a domed roof as pivot for a 'Flying Wraparound Kick' aimed at the chasing soldiers.

LEAP OF FAITH
A leap can surprise the enemy, and when Dastan meets Tamina's bodyguard Asoka, he jumps so high that he pulls the startled Alamutian off his horse.

LIVE AND KICKING
Dastan can use his skill in hand-to-hand combat. When attacked by Garsiv at Avrat, Dastan is able to spin around, push off, and virtually floor his brother with a kick to the head.

NASAF

RISING OUT OF THE DESERTS, THE FAMOUS CITY OF Nasaf is dominated by Sharaman's huge palace, which towers above the red roofs. Hot, dirty and over-crowded, Nasaf is bursting with life. From the nobles hanging round the palace, to the Silk Road traders in the marketplace, to the orphans who live in the garbage dumps, Nasaf reflects the many faces of Persia. This city of contrasts has slums and temples, fortresses and ruins, busy thoroughfares and dingy alleys. However, it is also the seat of power, and with the royals, the military and the government officials ever-present, Nasaf truly feels like the capital city of Persia.

SILK CITY
Nasaf lies right on the Silk Road so the marketplace is always packed with stores whose tables and shelves are heavy with exotic goods from the East and the West.

HIGH RISE
As Nasaf is built upon a hill with the palace at its highest point, it means the royal seat is visible for miles around – a reminder to all of the King's authority.

TENT TOWN

Sometimes hundreds of nomadic Bedouin set up camp outside the city walls, swelling Nasaf's population with a temporary shanty-town made from tents.

THE ROYAL PALACE

So much history has taken place at the royal Palace – Sharaman's coronation, the birth of Tus and Garsiv – but it is later where the King spends a lot of time in contemplative prayer.

PRINCE TUS

AS SHARAMAN'S ELDEST SON, TUS IS THE CROWN Prince of Persia and the heir to the throne. Dedicated, diplomatic and desperate not to mess up, Tus has all the right qualities to be king but not the confidence – yet. Believing in the importance of following protocol, Tus respects the royal rules and traditions of Persia. This sensible side to his character is a strength that will help the future stability of Persia. He may come across as more serious and uptight than his brothers, but in reality Tus is a tower of strength who frequently acts as peacemaker when the headstrong Garsiv and Dastan argue.

BATTLING NERVES

As a taster of what is to come, Sharaman gives Tus the responsibility of being in charge of the armies waiting to attack Alamut. As the Prince still feels he needs to prove himself, he anxiously fingers his amber prayer beads before ordering battle to commence. Deep down, however, he is more than capable of leading the forces of Persia.

ROYAL DELEGATION

Tus is acutely aware that he is not yet ready to rule, so the cautious Crown Prince likes to listen to the opinions of others before making important decisions. Ultimately, impressionable Tus does not trust his own judgement so he relies on the counsel of other family members, which leaves him open to the influence of his evil uncle.

TAKING THE REIGNS

The day after his father is murdered, Tus is thrust into the spotlight when he is proclaimed king. Battling through his grief, the reluctant ruler rises to the occasion by acting with authority. Sending out a message to all corners of the Kingdom, he raises the bounty on Dastan's head, and confidently declares 'our Empire remains stable, in the hands of a strong leader.'

SHARAMAN'S SECOND SON, GARSIV, WAS BORN TO be a warrior. His fingers itching to grab the hilt of his sword, Garsiv gets impatient during peacetime and is happiest when he is carrying out his role as the General of the Armies of Persia. More than just a little competitive, he is determined to prove to the king that he has the best military mind and muscle of the three Princes. Thankfully, battle-eager Garsiv is also a gifted soldier, and can land a deadly blow with his sword. He knows he will probably never be king, which may be just as well because the hot-headed warrior does not have the patience to rule Persia. However, he is exceptionally loyal to both his family and the Kingdom, and is very proud of their achievements – particularly if they are his own!

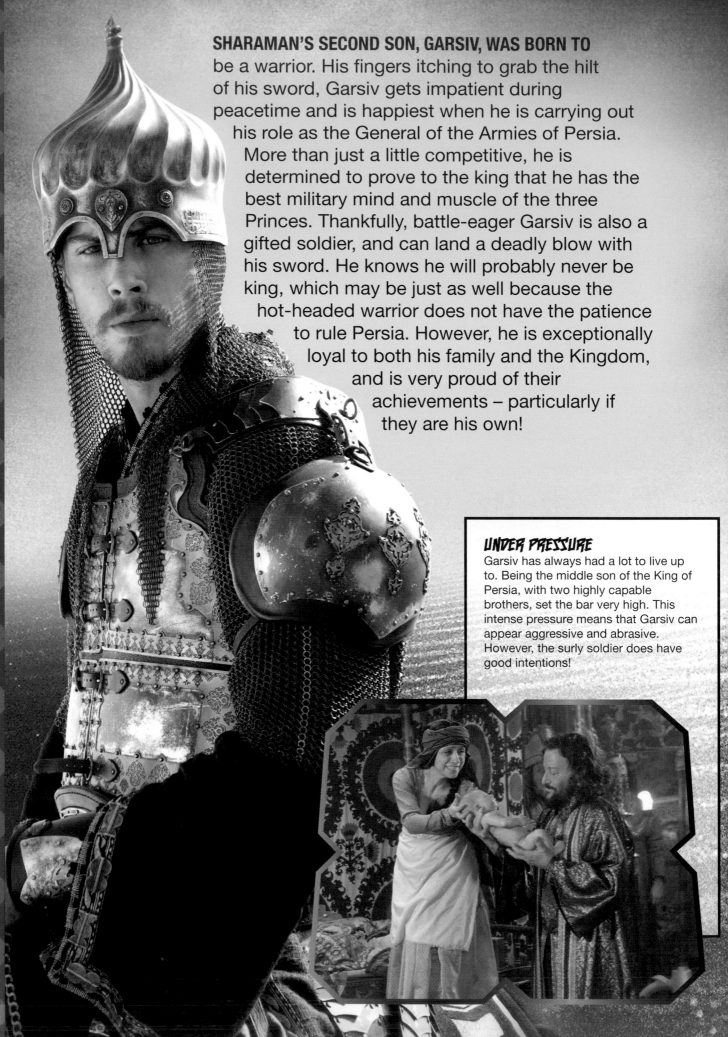

UNDER PRESSURE
Garsiv has always had a lot to live up to. Being the middle son of the King of Persia, with two highly capable brothers, set the bar very high. This intense pressure means that Garsiv can appear aggressive and abrasive. However, the surly soldier does have good intentions!

BROTHERLY LOVE?

Whilst Garsiv always looks up to Tus, he sometimes looks down on Dastan. He regards his younger brother as a loose cannon who doesn't always follow the rules. The rivalry between easily-riled Garsiv and relaxed Dastan has led to occasional personality clashes.

THE KING IS DEAD

Garsiv loved and respected his father. He is devastated when the King is murdered. Overwhelmed with feelings of revenge, it is no surprise that he immediately points the finger of suspicion at Dastan and gives chase. Garsiv has a tendency to jump to conclusions and act before thinking things through.

THE POWER OF THREE

King Sharaman declared that the love and loyalty between the three brothers is 'the sword that defends our empire.' The family ties between the brothers are strengthened by the affection they share for their father, as well as their adherence to the Kingdom's code of honour.

KING SHARAMAN IS DIRECTLY DESCENDED FROM the great King Ardishar who ruled Persia from 208 CE. Ardishar was the first King of the Sassanid dynasty and unified many of Persia's borders through military campaigns to create a large empire which included present-day Iran, Afghanistan, Iraq and most of Turkey, among others. Sharaman is a peaceful king who desires security for Persia and hopes that he can achieve this during his reign with the help of his loyal sons.

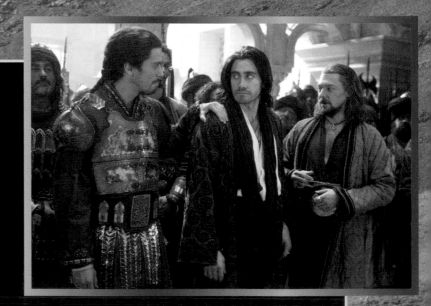

NOBLE INHERITANCE

With male heirs, the continuance of the royal bloodline is guaranteed. Within royal tradition, there is the assumption that certain noble qualities are carried in the genes. However, this is challenged by the fact that Dastan is not a blood relation yet shows great nobility of spirit and Nizam is of royal blood and he is anything but noble.

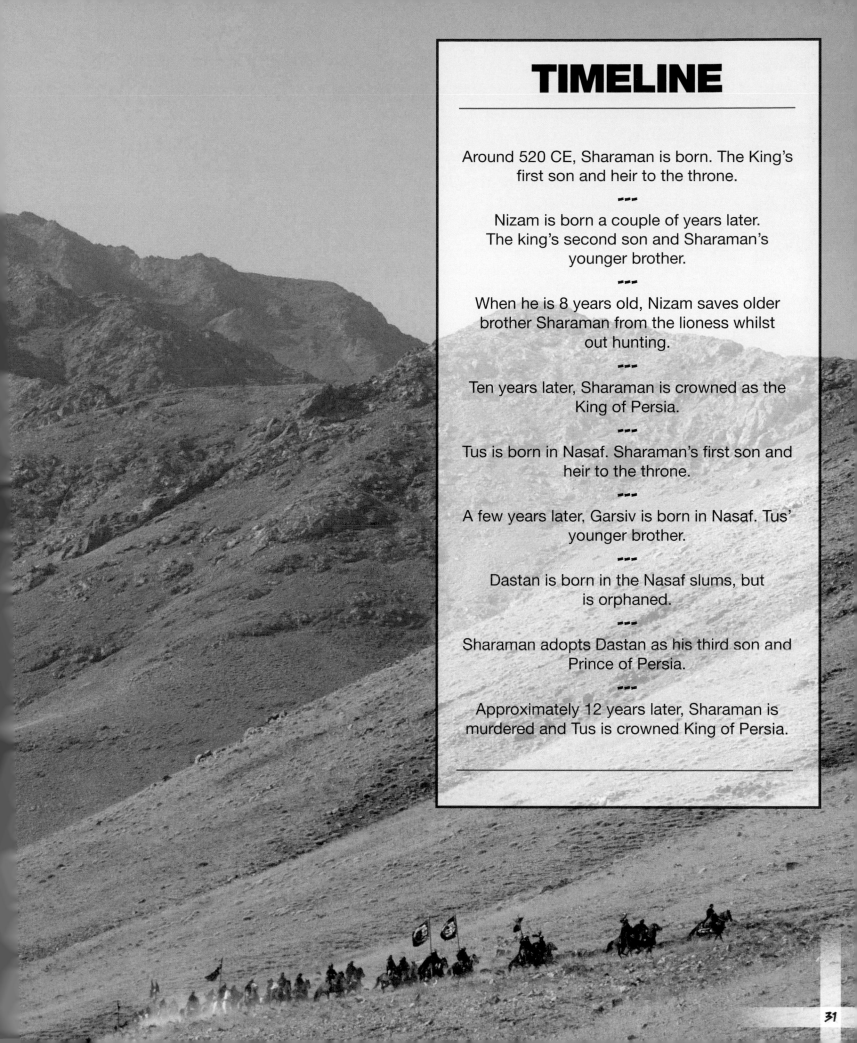

TIMELINE

Around 520 CE, Sharaman is born. The King's first son and heir to the throne.

Nizam is born a couple of years later. The king's second son and Sharaman's younger brother.

When he is 8 years old, Nizam saves older brother Sharaman from the lioness whilst out hunting.

Ten years later, Sharaman is crowned as the King of Persia.

Tus is born in Nasaf. Sharaman's first son and heir to the throne.

A few years later, Garsiv is born in Nasaf. Tus' younger brother.

Dastan is born in the Nasaf slums, but is orphaned.

Sharaman adopts Dastan as his third son and Prince of Persia.

Approximately 12 years later, Sharaman is murdered and Tus is crowned King of Persia.

ALAMUT

THE SPECTACULAR SACRED CITY OF ALAMUT RISES sharply out of a valley on the Persian border. Protected by awe-inspiring high walls that have not been penetrated for over a thousand years, the magnificent marble buildings and elaborate towers are decorated with ornate detail, and jostle for space with exotic vegetation. Alamut has enjoyed great wealth from its trading connections, and its status as a cultural and religious centre. But the city has concealed an incredible secret since its foundation. Alamut sits directly on top of the Sandglass of Time!

CITY STREETS
The abundance of fine buildings lining every Alamutian street is partly due to riches from the city's proximity to the Silk Road, and partly due to its neutrality which has kept it free of invaders.

OPEN SPACE
The citizens of Alamut love their city. The whole place has been carefully constructed to give stunning views from every vantage point, whether looking up from a square or looking down from a tower.

THE HIGH TEMPLE

The mysterious High Temple sits right on top of the city, its tip sometimes shrouded in clouds. It is the holiest place in Alamut and where the Princess prays when the Persians attack.

THE CITY WALLS AND EASTERN GATE

The vertigo-inducing city walls are well-defended with vats of boiling oil poured onto anybody foolish enough to try scaling them! When Dastan succeeds he opens the Eastern Gate to allow the Persians in.

THE LEGENDARY ROYAL PALACE IS THE HEART of Alamut. With its beautifully crafted golden dome, tremendous turrets and ornate interior, every inch of the building has been finished in perfect detail to reflect the importance of the royal family and the city's devotion to the gods. One of the finest buildings in the entire region, the Palace is intended to strike awe into and move all those who enter it. For Tamina, it is not only a symbol of the city's greatness, but is also the place she grew up and where she will rule from when she comes of age.

THE GRAND HALL
The enormous grand hall is the official place for major functions, although it was never intended to hold a banquet to honour an invading Persian King!

THE PALACE STEPS
Many foreign dignitaries and religious leaders have made their way into the palace up the famous steps. It is the first close up view any visitor gets of the palatial complex.

ROYAL BALCONY

The royal balcony provides a vantage point to look across the valley. From here Tamina and her Regent can view the Persian army camped outside the city on the verge of attack.

SKY CHAMBER

The Palace of Alamut is very high. The Sky Chamber lets the light flood in and gives anyone in it the sense of being amongst the clouds.

THE LEGEND OF THE GUARDIANS

MANY YEARS AGO, THE WORLD WAS RIDDLED WITH avarice and torn asunder with treachery. The gods looked down on the world they had created and decided enough was enough. They sent a terrifying sandstorm to obliterate mankind, and in the wake of its terrifying path of destruction only one girl survived. The girl made a journey to plead with the gods to give mankind another chance, offering her life in exchange. Impressed by the purity of her spirit and reminded that man could do good, they granted her wish and returned humankind to the world, in turn creating the legacy of the Guardians.

THROUGH THE GENERATIONS

As a direct descendent of the original girl who survived the gods' sandstorm, Princess Tamina is the current Guardian. The legends, secrets and responsibilities of the Guardians have passed from generation to generation partly through the bloodline of the Alamutian royal family, defining virtually everything they do.

THE SANDGLASS AND THE DAGGER

The gods created an enormous sandglass beneath Alamut to encase all the Sand of Time from the storm. If the sand were ever to be released, the resulting storm would end in apocalypse for the world. To help protect the Sandglass the gods created a Dagger of Time which could reverse time for short periods, but could also pierce the Sandglass. The Guardians must protect the sandglass and ensure the Dagger never falls into the wrong hands.

TAMINA, THE BEAUTIFUL PRINCESS OF ALAMUT, is committed to carrying out her royal and religious duties. Brought up with her city's traditions and teachings, Tamina knows the responsibilities that come with both the position of Princess, and her role as one of the Guardians. Clever, conscientious and courageous, Tamina is fiercely loyal to the people of Alamut, who love and respect her in return. She isn't timid and is never afraid to speak her mind, especially if it upsets Dastan and the Persians! With her aristocratic upbringing, the Princess is well-educated and cultured, but sometimes can look down on those less refined than her. Naturally, she regards Dastan and the invading Persian Army as ill-mannered oafs!

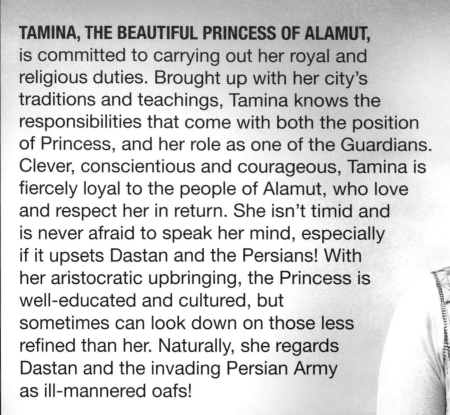

TAMINA'S TEAM

With an entourage attending to her needs in her chambers, bodyguards in abundance and the sage guidance of the Regent of Alamut, the Princess is well protected by those surrounding her. Despite this, Tamina chooses not to hide herself away in the city's highest towers – she is worldly wise, in touch with the people and aware of the troubles they face.

HOLY ORDERS

Ultimately, all of Tamina's actions are guided by her belief in the gods. As one of the Guardians, her sacred duty is to protect the Dagger and the Sandglass. Evoking the power of the gods through prayer and song, Tamina is aware of what she must do. She tells Dastan 'I know what the gods have asked of me. I will fulfil that calling, no matter the consequences.'

YOUR TURN TO WAIT

The Princess has been served by subjects all her life in sumptuous surroundings. But the tables are turned when she is briefly forced to dress as a waitress after Dastan sells her to Sheikh Amar in the Valley of the Slaves. Tamina is not too happy at suffering this indignity, and she doesn't even get the chance to collect any tips!

IN DISGUISE

When the Dagger of Time is in danger of falling into the wrong hands, the Princess proves she can act under pressure. Always agile and alert, the Princess's quick wits are put to the test when she has to help Dastan escape from Alamut. Her feisty attitude pays off and Dastan seems impressed.

THOUSANDS OF YEARS AGO THE GODS CREATED the Dagger of Time to help protect the Sandglass of the Gods, but also to test whether mankind would be tempted to misuse the ancient artifact. When the bearer of the Dagger presses down on the jewel on the hilt it releases a small quantity of the mysterious glowing sand, which swirls inside the glass handle. Time can then be reversed for up to one minute, with only the bearer of the Dagger being aware of this shift. Once the Dagger's handle is empty it can only be refilled with the magical sand from the Sandglass, although Princess Tamina keeps a small quantity hidden. The Dagger also masks an even bigger secret – it is the only object that can pierce the Sandglass.

The crystal hilt is full of the mystical glowing sand swirling round and round.

By pressing down on the red jewel some of the sand will be released from the hilt.

The dagger can only hold enough temporal sand to reverse time for one minute.

'Our Lives are forever in the hands of the gods'

The inscription reminds the bearer of their mission and their duty to the gods.

The innocuous cloth that the dagger's wrapped in is designed to disguise its great importance.

GUARDED BY THE GUARDIAN

After they created it at the Hidden Valley, the gods entrusted the Dagger to the first Guardian. Successive generations of Guardians have kept it safe at Alamut ever since. The consequences of it falling into the wrong hands are too awful to contemplate, and the current Guardian, Tamina, will protect the Dagger whatever it takes. However, there is always another option – to take the Dagger back to the Hidden Valley where it was first received, and return it to the gods for good.

ON THE RUN

AFTER TAMINA HELPS DASTAN FLEE FROM ALAMUT, she then tries to get the Dagger by attempting to kill Dastan. During the attack the Prince accidentally activates the Dagger, reverses time, and saves himself. With this new knowledge, Dastan is sure that Tus killed the King, and the young prince resolves to travel to Avrat for the King's funeral to tell Nizam his suspicions. However, the best route to Avrat is through the dangerous Valley of the Slaves. Tamina is scared of the journey, but doesn't want to be left alone in the desert. Now the two are in a cat and mouse game to outwit each other – he can't trust her, and she wants the Dagger!

THE DESERT TRACK

Although Tamina and Dastan are on the run, it is difficult to hurry in the desert. Progress is slow but steady due to the searing heat and sand and rock underfoot. Fortunately they have Aksh, the finest horse in the Kingdom, to accompany them. Unfortunately, they have disguised themselves as Berbers, and their clothes reek of camel's urine!

ON A KNIFE EDGE

The Dagger of Time sparks some sharp exchanges between the Prince and Princess. He senses she's not telling the whole truth and wants to know if she has any of the magical sand to refill it. Tamina won't tell Dastan her secrets and keeps on mocking him. However, their insult-trading comes to an abrupt end when Tamina suddenly collapses from the heat.

JOIN THE CLUB

But the Princess's collapse is a trick! She clubs Dastan over the head with a skeleton bone and knocks him out cold, grabs the dagger and rides off on Aksh. Tamina may have left him for dead, but Dastan wakes up very much alive and surrounded by Sheikh Amar's band of men in the Valley of the Slaves.

DEAL OR NO DEAL

Double-dealing Dastan manages to get one up on the Princess when he trades her to Sheikh Amar in return for the promise of supplies. But when Amar rounds them both up he realises they are royalty and threatens to turn them over to Tus.

IN EASTERN PERSIA LIES THE VALLEY OF THE Slaves – a barren and desolate dustbowl inhabited by marauding gangs of murderous thieves and outlaw – a place so dangerous it must be avoided at all costs! Cut deep into the earth from the old salt mines, the place became chaotic and lawless when the slaves overthrew their masters. Or so it would seem! In fact, the story is a pack of lies concocted by the shady Sheikh Amar to keep visitors away so he can continue his own gambling and black-market operations undisturbed!

DRY AS A BONE
The sinister skeletons at the Valley entrance are designed to deter terrified travellers from entering. They were placed there by Sheikh Amar, who bought them as a job lot from a gypsy market!

AMAR'S ARMY
The Valley is patrolled and controlled by men loyal to Sheikh Amar. Although they do keep some semblance of order, their main aim is to keep the authorities out – particularly tax inspectors!

DESERTED!
After Tamina has abandoned Dastan, he wakes up surrounded by Amar's men. He is amazed that they are not bloodthirsty bandits, but are prepared to cut a deal as long as they make a profit!

VALLEY OF THE KNAVES
The roguish ruler of the Valley of the Slaves is really Sheikh Amar. He's turned a place with nothing much going for it, into a place with nothing much going for it, but that makes him money!

SHEIKH AMAR

AS THE SELF-STYLED LEADER OF THE VALLEY OF THE Slaves, Sheikh Amar is crafty, conniving, and rather crooked. Amar used to be a slave in the salt-mines until the owner died and the fake Sheikh saw an opportunity to grab power. Spreading false stories that the Valley is over-run with murderous savages has kept the authorities and tax inspectors at bay. Amar has managed to establish his own empire of dodgy dealings, illegal operations and rigged ostrich races that have made the unscrupulous entrepreneur a rich man. And with just the right level of charm, this chancer always seems to be able to pull off the right deal and dodge the dreaded tax inspectors!

THE LOW DOWN
It's not always advisable to do business with Amar. Usually one step ahead, the shifty Sheikh won't hesitate to make them break a deal if there is money to be made. When Dastan lowers himself to Amar's level by doing a deal for Tamina, he is soon double-crossed. Realising the Prince's true identity, Amar intends to turn him over to Tus for the reward money.

HONOUR AMONGST THIEVES

Sheikh Amar is a charismatic leader who commands loyalty from his followers. Luckily for Amar, many of the slaves freed from the salt mines have stuck with him. They keep outsiders away, allowing him to coordinate his clandestine activities. With loyal head warrior Seso, Amar has found a best friend whom he highly respects.

THE PRICE OF A PRINCESS

For the Sheikh, every person has their price, and a princess is no exception. When he swaps Tamina for some supplies with Dastan, he even comments that she is worth about two camels! However, the Sheikh gets his just desserts when the Princess, working as a lowly waitress serving fermented milk at the ostrich races, sparks a riot and escapes!

LOSING THE DAGGER

After the Hassansins attack, Tamina and Dastan steal back the Dagger of Time from Sheikh Amar. Tamina promises the greedy Sheikh gold if he helps them deliver it to safety, appealing to his entrepreneurial spirit.

MEET THE OSTRICHES
The ostriches are kept in their holding pen between races. When they get going, they can reach speeds of up to 72 km per hour (45 miles per hour). In Persia they are also a source of food and feathers.

RAMSHACKLE RACETRACK
The rickety track itself is carved into the entrance of the old salt mine within the Slave Valley. The venue might not be the grandest, but they are almost always guaranteed a full house.

THERE IS NOT MUCH TO DO IN THE DESERT, AND in the Valley of the Slaves just about the only form of entertainment is gambling on the ostrich races run by Sheikh Amar. Twice a week, outlaws and vagrants flock from miles around to have a flutter on these flightless birds. However, the biggest winner is always the Sheikh, who has made the racing a lucrative money-spinner. The biggest losers are probably the riders. As they fly round the track they need to hold on tight to the ostrich, otherwise they end up with a mouthful of sand!

STICKING THEIR NECKS OUT
They stampede, squabble and jostle for position – and that's the crowd, not the ostriches. This loud and boisterous rabble, usually drunk on fermented milk, often ruffle each other's feathers!

HEAD IN THE SAND
The Sheikh runs the show and takes particular delight when his 'grand champion' star ostrich, Bethsheba, wins a race. Amar tries to disguise her ability so he can cunningly rig the results.

RIGHT-HAND MEN

EVERY TRUE HERO OR HEROINE NEEDS HELP ON THEIR adventures. Dastan, Tamina and Sheikh Amar all have fiercely loyal companions whom they trust with their lives. Not only do these sidekicks offer friendship, camaraderie and wise counsel but they are also prepared to make the ultimate sacrifice for their cause. By setting aside their own personal ambitions, they always act with duty and honour. In fact, many would give their right arm to have a right-hand man like Bis, Asoka or Seso!

BIS: NOBLE SOLDIER

Bis is Dastan's loyal lieutenant, conscientious confidant, and best friend. A skilled swordsman and soldier in Dastan's personal forces, Bis would die for the Prince. Bis is of noble birth and wears the robes to prove it. His background means he is more refined and less rebellious than the Prince, but despite these differences their bond is unbreakable.

ASOKA: TRUSTED BODYGUARD

Tamina's main bodyguard, Asoka is tasked with protecting the Princess. Showing remarkable devotion and dedication at all times, Asoka is regarded so highly by Tamina that she entrusts him to smuggle the Dagger of Time out of Alamut. Asoka is the strong silent type – he doesn't say much, preferring to let his incredible expertise with a scimitar do the talking!

SESO: HEAD WARRIOR

Once Seso's life was saved by Amar, he was indebted to the Sheikh for the rest of his days. As one of the Ngbaka people, and Head Warrior of the Valley of the Slaves, Seso has always acted with unswerving honour. Quiet and contemplative, Seso's prayers and meditations help him to throw his tri-blade knife with deadly accuracy, as well as earn Amar's respect.

51

THE HASSANSINS

THE HASSANSINS ARE A MYSTERIOUS AND sinister cult of cold-hearted killers. With pure evil intent, these monstrous characters feel nothing, all humanity stripped away by the teachings of their upbringing and their abominable actions. For years, Persian royalty had silently used these shadowy figures to carry out assassinations, but Sharaman stopped the practise and outlawed the cult. Seizing the opportunity, Nizam secretly kept a few of the most dangerous and vicious Hassansins to help him achieve his own evil end-game. Now Dastan and Tamina find themselves pitted against Zolm and his Hassansins!

ZOLM (LEAD HASSANSIN)

With a name meaning 'cruelty' and his chilling pale blue eyes, Zolm is the terrifying head Hassansin. Usually choosing to attack with pit vipers, Zolm leads the other Hassansins into battle with eerie silence. He is also the main point of contact with Nizam. He is the one who lets the Vizier know about the ultimate secret of the Sands of Time.

BELIEFS

The Hassansins turned to the dark side many years ago. They propagated their existence by training themselves in janna–the ancient art of killing quickly. From young boys they have been fed opiates to numb their souls, and in their smoke-filled trances they see visions of death which help them carry out their crimes.

The pit vipers are an important symbol in the Hassansins' beliefs, but once they have been charmed, they also act as a lethal weapon launched from their sleeves.

TAMAH (RAZOR-GLOVE)

Tamah, meaning 'greed,' wears a pair of lethal gloves covered in very long razor blades, which he uses in combat to slash and gut his victims.

SETAM (PORCUPINE)

Setam, meaning 'tyranny,' is a human porcupine. With his armour covered in needle-sharp spikes, he's said to have 'eyes of coal' and 'skin creased as the desert.'

GHAZAB (DOUBLE- BLADED HALBERD)

Few survive when Ghazab, meaning 'wrath,' swings his halberd. A formidable opponent, he's one of three Hassansins to survive the fight at the Bottomless Well.

GOOL (SCIMITAR GIANT)

Gool is basically an orge – an enormous ghoul of a man – who fights with a colossal scimitar that can slice an opponent right in half.

NEFRAT (GREEK FIRE)

Nefrat, meaning 'hatred,' carries round a bandolier of Greek Fire Grenades in order to burn his enemies to ash in a flash of flames!

AKVAN (STALLION)

Akvan is the black stallion that Zolm rides. Like all the Hassansins' horses, Akvan has been specially trained, and wears terrifying spiked armour.

HASSAD (WHIP-BLADE)

Holding a deadly whip blade in each hand, Hassad can maim and kill his foes with alarming accuracy. His name means 'envy.'

IN THE PERSIAN EMPIRE, WEAPONRY PLAYS A BIG PART IN the way of life. With some warriors trying to enforce their law through the sword, and others defending themselves from danger, there are arms stockpiled throughout the land. While some soldiers are skilled with just a sword, others have developed expertise in a variety of more exotic weaponry. Whips, axes, clubs and crossbows are just some examples. Warriors have practised and practised, perfecting their savage specialism in preparation for battle. In particular, the individual Hassansins have mastered their art with deadly consequences!

DASTAN'S WEAPONS
Although he prefers hand-to-hand combat, Dastan has an armoury of different blades at his disposal. He is skilled with a sword and handy with a dagger, and will choose the right weapon for the right occasion. Tamina, too, has been known to use a dagger in a dangerous situation!

TAMINA'S CEREMONIAL DAGGER
Tamina doesn't always use her concealed ceremonial dagger for ceremonies! It has an extremely sharp blade so she can protect and defend herself.

EAGLE-HEADED SWORD
The eagle's head on the hilt of the sword reminds the bearer of the bird of prey's hunting skills and the way it can swoop down on its prey with remarkable precision.

ORNATE SWORD
The intricate pattern on this weapon are a reflection of the craftsmanship which has gone into making it, and the high quality of the blade.

SERRATED SWORD
The razor sharp teeth on one side of this weapon are particularly lethal as they can shred the flesh of a victim upon contact!

THE HASSANSINS' WEAPONS

The Hassansins use of weaponry is particularly cruel and brutal. There is no honour or code of conduct in the way they fight. They have been trained to kill as quickly as possible and their armoury is designed accordingly, with blades and spikes so sharp they can maim and kill instantly, slicing through human flesh and bone with ease.

TAMAH RAZOR GLOVES
When worn in battle, this pair of razor gloves is a deadly slashing machine that can slice a foe to shreds.

NEFRAT FIRE GRENADES
When thrown, the clay canister of a Greek Fire Grenade breaks open to splatter lethal liquid fire on the victim.

HASSAD'S BLADED WHIPS
When two whip blades curl through the air with deadly precision, a limb can easily be severed clean from a person's body.

GOOL'S SCIMITAR
Gool's giant scimitar is so large it can almost shut out the sun. Most men flee just on glimpsing the blade!

SETAM'S SPIKES
Setam's needle-sharp spikes can puncture the body right into the bone. They are worn on armour, but can also be thrown.

FUNERAL IN AVRAT

IN THE HALLOWED TRADITION OF THE burial of Kings of Persia, King Sharaman's funeral is held at the Holy City of Avrat. With dozens of foreign dignitaries in attendance, thousands of wailing mourners and worshippers flock to the narrow city streets to pay their last respects. The funeral procession passes through the city's Leopard Gates, and ends up at the Tomb of Kings, where various mausoleums dedicated to generations of late Persian Kings have been carved into the cliff face. Each tomb is painstakingly crafted by hundreds of men, creating a place reflecting the reverence and devotion shown to each King.

IN DISGUISE

Tamina and Dastan flee the Valley of the Slaves to attend the funeral at Avrat and to try and confront Nizam. The pair disguise themselves. Dastan is one of the exhausted porters carrying a very heavy Mughal Sultan upon an ivory platform. Tamina is a patient waitress holding a basket of black walnuts for the Sultan to guzzle on. In those lowly positions, no one is going to guess they are royalty!

THE MOMENT OF TRUTH

By secretly slipping him a note, Dastan is able to arrange a meeting with Nizam at the bazaar at Avrat. Whilst protesting his innocence, Dastan notices that Nizam's hands are burnt. He suddenly realises that Nizam must have handled the poisoned clock that murdered the King. Putting two and two together, he realises the truth of his uncle's treachery.

ONLY A HANDFUL OF PEOPLE KNOW ITS SECRET.
And even fewer have seen it! The astonishing
Sandglass of the Gods lies in an enormous
chamber directly underneath the Royal Palace
at Alamut. The huge hourglass was created by
the gods to encase the Pure Sand from the
apocalyptic storm originally sent to destroy
mankind. The Sandglass is an overwhelming
reminder of the power of the gods and the
fragility of the fate of mankind. If the sand
were ever to be released, humanity would
be obliterated.

*The eerie glow of tons and tons of
strange, swirling sand illuminates the
cavern around it, lighting the stone
bridge which spans the chamber, and
seeping into the surrounding labyrinth.*

STABBING THE SANDGLASS

The Dagger of Time is the only object that can pierce the Sandglass. The effect of this depends very much on the intentions of the bearer of the dagger. If they are evil then the sandglass will crack, Pure Sand pouring out with cataclysmic consequences – the destruction of mankind! The question is, can Dastan and Tamina stop Nizam?

GETTING READY FOR BATTLE AND PUTTING ON THE right gear is a vital ritual for any warrior. Not only does the equipment have to be light enough to allow flexible movement but it also has to be able to protect the person from the heavy blow of a sharp blade. Usually made from iron and hide, having the right armour and clothing can mean the difference between life and death. Battle gear is also a uniform that reflects both rank and loyalties. A soldier needs to make sure he can clearly identify whose side he is on so he is only attacked by your enemies!

AKSH

A horse is crucial for success in battle, and is also an important status symbol. Aksh is easily the finest horse in Persia and has already been ridden by the King into battle. After the Persian army's success at Alamut, Sharaman gives Aksh to Garsiv as a gift. However, the Prince is absolutely livid when Dastan steals Aksh when he flees the city!

GARSIV

As a competitive Prince who takes his war-craft seriously, Garsiv always wears top-of-the-range gear.

Protective shoulder armour made out of iron.

Breastplate armour protects the vital organs of the heart and lungs.

Lightweight tunic to ease body movement and keep the body cool.

The design on Garsiv's trousers indicates his high army ranking.

ZOLM

Being a Hassansin, Zolm is in a perpetual state of conflict, so he's always dressed to be battle-ready.

ASOKA

Reflecting their neutrality, the Alamutian battle dress is more ceremonial than that of the Persian Army.

As a royal bodyguard, Asoka's armour has to he thoroughly polished.

Black headscarf provides protection from the scorching sun.

Cream tunic coordinates with the Alamutian gold armour.

Metallic chain vest provides protection from blades, but is also very light.

Zolm's cape is black, the Hassansins' colour of choice.

Wrist support bracelets provide protection and helps Asoka use heavy weapons.

Trouser guard helps Asoka avoid those particularly painful blows.

Tight belt to hold Zolm's dagger.

Asoka's army boots are made out of hide.

THE LUSH VEGETATION, SHELTERED CLIMATE AND
sheer serenity of the incredible Hidden Valley
is a reward for the eyes of weary travellers
who have journeyed through the inhospitable
tundra of the foothills of the Himalayas and the
frozen Ice Forest. Known only to very few and
being the final destination of the original path
of the Guardians, the Valley contains the secret
Temple of Water. This is where the Dagger of
Time can be returned to the gods, but only
at the cost of the life of one of the Guardians.
Accessible through a concealed fissure in the
rock and protected by a small settlement, the
temple is located in a cavern which is cold,
dank and flowing with snowmelt.

THE DAGGER AND THE CREVICE

Located at the back of the temple is the crevice where the Dagger of Time may be returned by a Guardian, at the very spot where it was originally delivered by the gods. When Tamina and Dastan travel through the Hidden Valley to the cave they endeavor to return the Dagger to the crevice, but at the last minute the Hassansins attack and the Dagger goes missing.

THE SAND ROOM

UNDERNEATH THE PALACE AT ALAMUT AND SURROUNDING
the Sandglass is a sand room. Built by the Guardians
to stop anybody stumbling across the Sandglass, only
very few know the safe way through. When the gods
discover their sacred space has been violated, they
decide on a little earthquake as an indication of their
anger. With the ground disappearing beneath Dastan's
feet, this proves to be the toughest test of physical
ability and mental agility he has faced – and the biggest
battle of nerves!

As the sand drains rapidly from the
chamber, it is clear how far the
foundations of the bridge stretch down
below. Initially, these give a lifeline for
Dastan who lands on them using his
acrobatic skills.

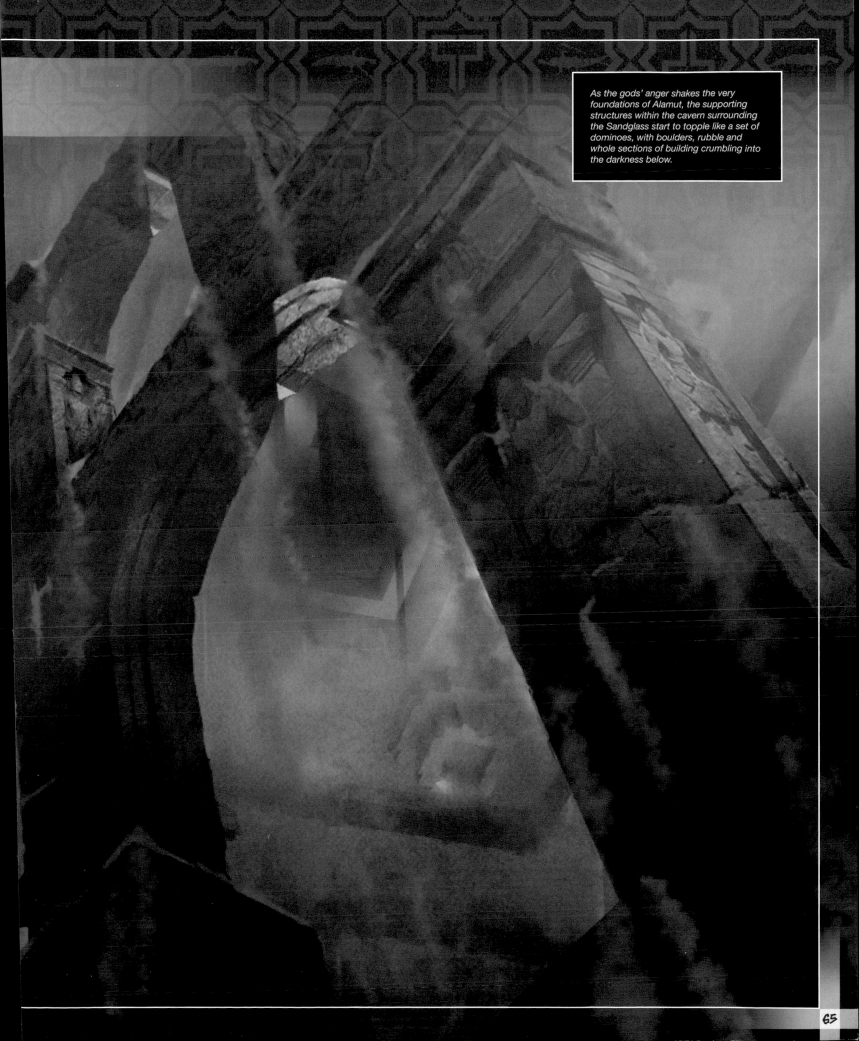

As the gods' anger shakes the very foundations of Alamut, the supporting structures within the cavern surrounding the Sandglass start to topple like a set of dominoes, with boulders, rubble and whole sections of building crumbling into the darkness below.

TAMINA AND DASTAN

HE WAS BORN AND RAISED LIVING ON THE streets, while she has enjoyed a privileged upbringing. He thinks she is disrespectful, while she thinks he has the manners of a camel and is not pleased that he has just invaded her city. On the face of it, they may appear to be very different, but Dastan and Tamina also share some of the same resilience, spirit and sense of honour. As destiny forces their paths to cross, they must get to know each other better.

CHEMISTRY?

When Dastan first sees Tamina in the High Template at Alamut, he is struck silent by how beautiful she is. Unfortunately, she is not so impressed! When he fetches her from her chambers to present to King Sharaman, not only does she accuse him of being 'senseless and brutal,' she also calls him 'thick-headed!'

A DATE WITH A DAGGER

After his skirmish with Asoka, Dastan gains the Dagger of Time, the one object that Tamina is desperate to prevent getting into the wrong hands. When Tamina notices that the Prince has the mysterious weapon, it means she must stay with him until she finds the right time to outwit him, snatch it back, and escape.

RULES OF ENGAGEMENT

When Tus first sees Tamina he wants to make her one of his wives. Confiding in Dastan, he makes his younger brother promise to present Tamina to his father, but also kill the Princess if Sharaman does not approve of his plan. To everybody's surprise, Sharaman suggests that Tamina should be betrothed to Dastan rather than Tus!

DIVULGING IN THE DESERT

As Tamina and Dastan bicker their way through the desolate desert landscape on the way to Avrat, they both succeed in outsmarting the other to control the Dagger. Despite this, negotiating the harsh terrain seems to pull them together. Tamina realises how honourable Dastan really is, and tells him the truth about the Dagger's power and her higher mission.

STRONG BOND

It is clear that there has always been some chemistry between the Prince and Princess, but as their adventures have continued they have become closer and closer. In some respects, they have seen the best and worst of each other, and from this a mutual respect and a good friendship has emerged. But just how strong is it?

THE END GAME

TIME IS RUNNING OUT FOR DASTAN TO PROVE his own innocence to Garsiv and Tus, the newly crowned King of Persia. Finally catching up with his eldest brother at Alamut, Dastan needs to demonstrate the powers of the Dagger of Time and explain its greater significance with the Sandglass. Even harder, he needs to persuade Tus that Nizam is the guilty party and must be stopped, whatever the consequences.

THE FINAL FIGHT

But it may be too late. Under the pretense of searching for secret weapon forges in Alamut, Nizam's cronies have located the entrance to the secret complex of caverns and passages that lead to the Sandglass. With Nizam and his Hassansins hell bent on taking back the Dagger, it may allow Nizam to pierce the Sandglass and bring the total destruction of mankind! Only Dastan and Tamina have what it takes to stop them.

INDEX

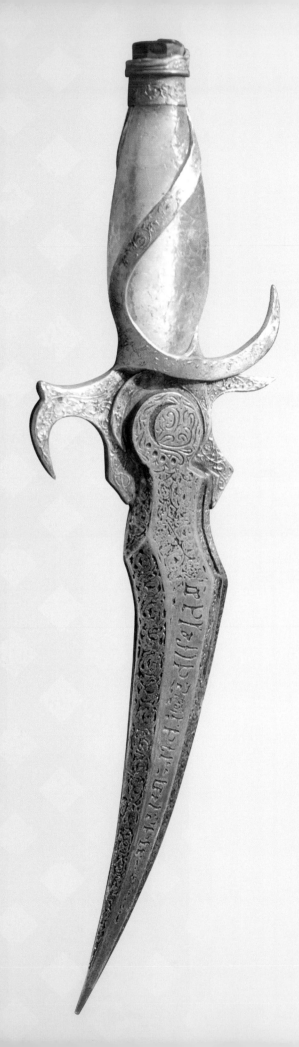

LONDON, NEW YORK, MUNICH
MELBOURNE AND DELHI

Editor Victoria Taylor
Senior Designer Nathan Martin
Managing Editor Catherine Saunders
Publishing Manager Simon Beecroft
Category Publisher Alex Allen
Production Editor Siu Chan
Print Production Nick Seston

First published in Great Britain in 2010 by
Dorling Kindersley Limited,
80 Strand, London, WC2R 0RL

10 11 12 13 14 10 9 8 7 6 5 4 3 2 1
176417—02/10

Based on the screenplay written by Doug Miro & Carlo Bernard
From a screen story by Jordan Mechner and Boaz Yakin
Executive Producers Mike Stenson, Chad Oman, John August, Jordan
Mechner, Patrick McCormick, Eric McLeod
Produced by Jerry Bruckheimer
Directed by Mike Newell

A CIP catalogue record for this book
is available from the British Library.

ISBN: 978-0-7566-5763-5

Reproduced by Alta Images, London
Printed at TBB

DK would like to thank:
Chelsea Nissenbaum, Shiho Tilley, Elizabeth Rudnick,
Doug Bantz, Jon Rogers and Erik Schmudde at Disney Publishing,
and Lindsay Kent and Jo Casey for their editorial assistance.

Discover more at
www.dk.com

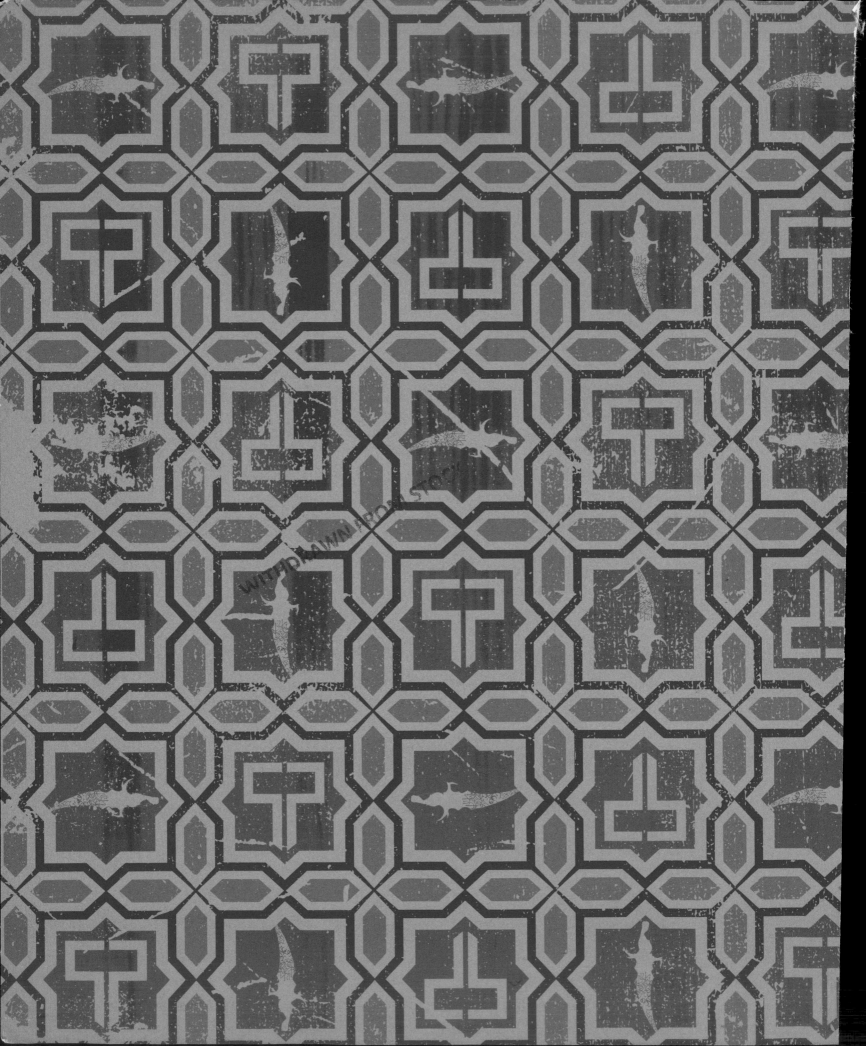